Questions

Directions to Who You Are

TIM W. TURNER

www.questionsthebook.com

Be a person

who knew

yesterday

that

today

would be

special.

Introduction

Life

It began as a violent, volcanic wind.
Relentless rain swept the planet that has become our home.

It was an earth with growing pains, in a hurry to mature.
It shook and trembled.
Mountains rose and valleys lay waiting for
streams and sunlight, for flowers-bees-butterflies.

Then a small creature began roaming the earth—man.
He walked—he thought—he planned—he survived.

Growth—reproduction—
each newborn somewhat like its parents—but different.
With each generation came the weak and the strong—
the givers and the takers—the excited and the bored.
Never do all groups walk entirely together.

Man: a traveler in time and space:

a blacksmith, a scientist, a poet, a painter, a man.

A creature set out to better himself by using

what was at his fingertips—the earth.

Time Passed

Time: man surviving and multiplying across the globe.

Time: man roaming the earth,

polluting streams and air, killing, surviving.

Time: man continuing to think, creating races, classes,

languages. Nomads—empires—civilizations—each racing to

make things different—to make things better.

Time: man traveling across the sea—across the earth

finding adventure and challenge.

Man: in a new home, free to do what was not allowed
where he came from—building and destroying once again.

Man: traveling, he came, saw, often defeating himself
without knowing.

Man: preserving himself and his actions—
writing—never forgetting.

Man: learning that with knowledge comes fear
through the lack of understanding.

Man: born to lead, to discover, to challenge.

Man: we have absorbed all traditions. We are what has passed,
and we look forward to what we will create for the future.

Forward

With the entire past in mind, **TODAY** arrives **Now!**

Today: You as you know you was yesterday.
Now it's today and you are more complex:
enjoyment more complex,
questions more complex,
answers more complex.

You've walked, run, crawled, jogged, even flown through life.
Blending get-up-and-go and relax-and-stop has
never caused any problems for you.

Days have turned into nights, months into years.
Wars have become peace—though fragile—and life is no more
difficult than you desire it to be.

You have lived comfortably in a very small, fast-moving world.
You may think of the past as "easy" and the future as uncertain.
Within memory, no change was unanimously accepted
but there have been changes.
Air and thoughts are being polluted.

Everything, including each of your minutes, is congested.
You have learned to treasure that which is rare.
And now such an infinite
number of truly important things
have become virtually extinct
you have much to search for.

Much of what you'll soon discover will be done
without the help of those you have
depended upon in the past.

Now: it happens, it's gone, it's past, it's history.
Another "**Now**" arrives—and a **Now**—and a **Now**—
until the average day for the average person
seems to apply to all—**Now.**

A series of all those **past "todays"**
leads us to the present.

This today consists of the
past, present, and **future.**
It's no different than **yesterday** or **tomorrow.**
But the Today of Now is truly not the same.

YOUR SERIES OF PAST TODAYS
LEAD US TO NOW

Today the sun rose and by mid-day warmed everything,
as only the sun can do.
Children swam; flowers bloomed—just an ordinary nice day.

Today the sun set—and the reds and oranges seemed
more beautiful than ever before—
a picture and a million words wrapped into one.
Today night blankets **everything**—a little at a time,
providing relief from the sun.

Today ends and something new appears—**Tomorrow.**

But that all took place a second ago—yesterday—
and you receive still another chance—another Today.

Today the sun had hardly enough intensity to be seen—as usual.
Today the sunset—it seemed earlier than usual—but you
didn't really notice. Today night appeared—nothing more.
And as a billion times before, the seconds tick past to another Today.

Today the sun did not shine.
No laughter was heard, no smiles were seen.
Today the night was our day.
But again, that was long ago—a second in the mind—yesterday.

We begin a new day—a day to ask questions—
a new very first day set in Total Darkness.
On a new Today, set in total darkness, people congregate
in groups—small in size but many in numbers.
One person—a Voice—not seen—is in charge.
It is a Voice to be heard—not as an instructor—just a **Voice.**

A Voice that speaks for all to hear.

A Voice that asks to hear questions from all.

A Voice that receives questions today and gives answers today.

A Voice that creates pictures in people's minds.

A Voice that tells tales, defines and states facts.
A Voice that answers your questions provided.
Each question is no longer than one word.

We are spoken to, we are told,
we each must ask one question today.

THE TODAY OF NOW
IS A TIME OF QUESTIONS

ALL WILL HEAR EACH QUESTION.

ALL WILL HEAR EACH ANSWER.

YOU MAY EACH ASK ONE QUESTION.

YOU MAY EACH SAY ONE WORD,
THOUGH ONLY ONE WORD.

And on a dark day—**Today—**
a day to start again,
Questions are asked
and answers are given.
All are present and all **listen—**
for there are **no distractions Today.**
And so we each ask our one question—
we each say our one word.

The First 52 Words

The First 52 Questions

Questions

Dark

The light of day casts across a valley of evergreens.

Small banks of clouds cover the surrounding hilltops.

In the valley several log buildings stand rugged

against the clear blue sky.

A clear mountain stream flows gently by.

You stand alone, in the midst of the valley.

At other times the air around you is heavy,

weighed down with uncertainty.

It surrounds you, purely dark and almost alive.

Things are happening around you—

some to the right—some to the left—some beneath you—

some way over your head.

Be a **positive** part of what's around you.
Never allow it to be too dark *for you to see.*

Every encounter with darkness
will make the light seem
brighter.

DARKNESS IS

A chance to ***smile***—and not be manipulated

A chance to *cry*—and not be pitied

A chance to ***think***—and not be diverted

A chance to ***die***—and be properly remembered

A chance to ***live***—and not be pressured

A chance for ***time***—to provide a moment to **dream**

A chance to ***see*** what's in your mind

A chance to ***brighten*** the world around you

There's a dark, faded border on the picture inside a silver frame.
The photo, clearly in focus, contains all the images
that make up the **greatness** of your life.

Silent

What are your reasons to be silent?

Because silence comes before speech

Because silence cradles the storms of existence

Because silence can be golden

Because silence can be trusted

Because silence can say more than spoken words

Because silence encourages others to explain

Because silence allows you to hear your own thoughts

Because silence shows respect for all around you

Because silence displays your wisdom

Because silence allows you to listen and learn

Because silence allows your heart and eyes to speak

What are your reasons to break the silence?

Because there is something to say

Because there is someone to say it to

Because there is someone to listen

Because there is someone to understand

Because there is someone to offer sympathy

Because there is someone to love each word

Because there is someone to hate each word

Because there is someone to benefit from your knowledge

Because when you're speaking others are not

Because you like to hear yourself talk

Because you can express your innermost feelings and desires

Because you must say what you really think.

Because when you speak you're creating the legacy of yourself

Today

I've got a feeling Today is the Day
Today is a stepping stone,
a learning experience that will
bring you closer to **who you are to be.**

Today—
Do everything you need to do to accomplish
everything you plan for tomorrow
Practice the things you learned yesterday
Be the person you've worked so long and hard to be

Today is
laughter, silence, belonging
planning and accomplishments
a rough winding road
a hill to climb
time filled with questions and answers that save time

Today is
a time for action
a time for inspiration
a day to be realistic
a day to follow your heart
a day to challenge your expectations
to fulfill your dreams

Today is
a day to be brave—to touch what is rare and real

Today
stay in touch with yourself—
guide yourself with conviction through the day—
take your time but be decisive

Today is
a day to follow straight lines
that bend with the wind

Today you should
give directions to those who are lost
make others better leaders
go for a walk
sing your song

Today you should
be saddened by the death of yesterday
make decisions—and move on
march in your own parade
hold the hand of someone in need
tell stories of what you've learned in the past
not expect worry to solve anything
travel slowly down one new road

Today is the tomorrow you planned for yesterday

Do

Do what your heart tells you

Do the very best you can

Do onto others

Do yourself a favor

Do something to surprise yourself

Do something that leads others in the right direction

Do something to fight evil

Do something to defend the defenseless

Do something that questions something that is beyond questioning

Do something that will generate feedback

Do something that reminds you that you're mortal

Do something that promotes happiness

Do something that creates a positive atmosphere

Do something that satisfies your curiosity

Do something that completes something

Do something that brings you peace and understanding

Do something that elevates you to a higher plateau

Do something that makes you happy

Do something that keeps you young

Do something that creates a better place to be

Things to Do

Look up an old friend

Reward yourself for a job well done

Hug someone who needs a hug

Love yourself

Laugh

Sit on the ground—
to get grounded

Get cozy

Exercise

Skip a rock

Climb to the top of a place that lets you see great distances

Concentrate on each task

Believe in yourself

Finish something you started

Arrange your priorities

Walk the beach

Make a wish

Do what others won't

Be a friend

Learn how to love

Design your tomorrow

Celebrate your victories

Look after those who need it

Go for a bike ride

Watch a bird glide on wind currents

Make love

Provide a way for those who are lost

Cry if you need to

Relax

Listen to your favorite music

Spend a minute staring at the full moon

Remember those who are gone

Dream while you're awake

Cherish your family

Paint a picture in your mind

Chat with those who need to be talked with

Build something

Make others feel important

Deceive the deceivers

Seize the moment

Learn

**Get in touch with the child within
as you approach new things.
Question, try, and learn
from new challenges.
Experience new ideas as
if you are a freshman, not a senior.**

Learn to look deep within yourself
Learn to make decisions
Learn to be wiser
Learn to teach
Learn to be available

Learn to breathe deeply
Learn to make time
Learn to walk at the right pace

Learn to feel important
Learn to have confidence

Learn to avoid obstacles
Learn to not hold a grudge
Learn to adjust

Learn to live beyond walls
Learn to travel uncharted waters
Learn to scratch beyond the surface
Learn to let your enthusiasm explode into your passion
Learn to have faith

Learn to truly care
Learn to bring positive sunlight into your heart
Learn to create what's needed

Learn to sacrifice

Learn to use your gifts

?Long

Be Patient
when long days allow a mist
to engulf you.
The sunlight will soon show you the way
to a place of balance.

Long shadows are cast
by those who stand up for what
they know is right.

There is a long road all must travel.
Be in touch with the hearts and spirits
of those who traveled the path before you.
They will guide you to secret places
and help you to see the mysteries of life.

It's been far too long since we—
Felt the positive effects of true love
Stopped to stare at a rainbow
Watched butterflies cross our path
Took a deep breath
Laughed out loud
Took second chances
Walked another road
Sang a new tune
Laid on our backs and looked up at the sky
Made a decent wish

It's been far too long since we—
Skipped a rock across the water
Watched the last five minutes of a sunset
Sat in the tall grass listening to the wind
Sailed away
Pondered the very best of times

It's been far too long since we—
Sat alone and allowed ourselves to dream
Took a long walk
Enjoyed a new friend
Enjoyed an old friend
Really got to know ourselves

True

Truth and wisdom
come in dreams.

Truth is one love,
which because of its existence
has built the
mightiest of monuments.

The truth is spoken by those
with the patience and spirit
to live on all sides of the triangle
that surrounds
the topic of their discussion.

Words that are false will tear at your skin;
words that are true will beat
deep within your heart.

You are true to yourself when—

You follow your heart

You speak quietly to yourself

You are kind to yourself

You allow yourself to be known for who you really are

You are responsive to the requests of others

**Your eyes see beyond the moods of others
and into their concerns**

You allow yourself to be flexible

You stand fully erect

You are true to yourself if—
you've done the best you know how under all circumstances
you are satisfied with yourself
you've borrowed no time not already paid for
you've abused no riches of real value

By rewarding yourself with the truth
you have bypassed mirrors that reflect no images.
You have missed nothing,
while avoiding some of those who misrepresent themselves.

Speak only of what is real.
It does not require hundreds of words to **speak the truth.**

Look

Look to yourself **to want nothing,**
seek nothing, depend on nothing—freedom.

Look **to the skies**—into faces—sense moods.

Look **into yourself.**
Where have you been? To get where?
Where are you now? To arrive where?
See yourself in the future recreated from events of the past.

Look **at the rain** building into streams.
Picture yourself traveling the adventure of each river—
maneuvering the roaring rapids.

Look **at your path**—on line—off course.
Stay close to yourself as you reach into your future.
Don't become lost during your search for yourself.

Look **behind** with each step you take—but only for a moment.
Recreate the past in your mind;
look at the why—the energy of how—the result of "done."
Many outcomes are grouped together to become your future.

Look **beyond** the walls around you
to find hidden treasures—
become your vision of the future.
Close your eyes—think deeply—
look down all the long corridors
and hidden passageways
leading to yourself.
Travel only those paths that are
cooled by fragrant breezes.

Look **at each second** as a miracle.

Look **to the world** as your library—
read every chapter of every book you touch.
Share what you learn.

Look at dreams in a big way, but keep them simple.

Look at your priorities.
Look at their order of importance each day.
Determine if something is out of place.

Look closely at your dreams.
Make them become real—one step at a time.

Look closely at what makes you happy.
Keep those thoughts with you every day.

Look for new paths to travel.
Enjoy the new sensations they bring to you, but watch your step.

Picture

A planet—**yours**—seen through
eyes from a distant place.

Eyes connected to wisdom and survival,
eyes fresh with the feeling of achievement,
eyes that never cry needlessly, eyes viewing you.

All scenes—all memories that are possible to view—
have now been tied together, creating you.

From time to time, for a moment,
you are the single most important event ever.

In the instant, you can **create**—or you can **destroy.**

Imagine all that is now—
able to exist another day—not able to exist another day.
It's your choice, a simple choice,
at the end of each of life's chapter another decision.
Forward—end.
As you make that decision, you'll plan tomorrow well—
live it fully—even plan for a next day.
You'll plan your future by planting the seeds for it now.
Close your eyes—imagine—taste—feel—touch—
listen to the pictures of your thoughts.
Love—wind—eyes—pain—heat—shame.

Picture yourself.
Hold out your hand. Kiss the air you breathe.

Grasp and hold on to all compassion and understanding.
Take in and store up the wisdom left behind
by those who lived and died while gathering it.

Picture a world *rich with the surroundings of creation,*
free to see the magnificent pictures supplied to you.

Never let yourself be occupied by a quest for destruction.
Let go of the you that is following.

Lead others through poisoned rain into fields of golden riches.
If your eyes see only worldly treasures, then be blind
just long enough to see the wonders that are invisible.

Paint pictures for future believers—
and believe in future images.

All these instructions have been heard before,
but never have the pictures been so obtainable.
The last picture is a view of the total end of everything;
that image must never be allowed to be developed.

As you discover your thoughts,
as one by one they come into focus,
and into your field of understanding,
you may realize and imagine the true colors of each—
their real meaning to you and the world.
Treasure the pictures you see, always search for new images.

Fear

No More Fear of—

Broken promises
Solitude
Exploration
Partial success
Asking questions
Cultural Differences
Things outside your zone

No More Fear of—

Second chances
Stretching goals
Showing emotion
Living dreams
The changes of age
Holding on too tight
Climbing to the top of obstacles
Displaying emotion
Love

No More Fear of—

Unwrapping your passion

Unopened packages

Giving your heart

Touching the meek

Needing seclusion

Your demise

Racing the wind

Obligation

No More Fear of—

Trusting everyone and everything possible

Displaying courage

Overachievement

The emergence of evil

Undistinguishable shadows

Lack of understanding

Spaces you do not recognize

Ideas not proven

Hidden memories

Activity beyond the routine

Deep water and dark spaces

The continuous construction of yourself

No More Fear of—Change

Noise?

**You may not speak with authority
in languages that are not yours.**

The sounds of your voice have been heard throughout time—
you are a part of all things everywhere.
The story of your place in time is spoken
by voices without volume in a tone heard
only by those closest to you.

The sounds of your lifetime have brought brightly colored gifts
to be placed at your feet—added love to your heart.
Your words exist in the dictionaries of every universal language.

Let your spirit whisper not shout.

The sounds of time are often noisy—
cluttered with moans and groans and annoyances.
***Your life has been provided to answer questions
not previously answered.***

The noises of the earth are absorbed by time—then packaged in small canisters marked "noises of life on earth." The canisters are then sent to an unknown far-off place where they might be analyzed at some later date. Try not to fill too many canisters.

Make the sounds of "you" forever—not part of any noise package. Their examination takes but a second—the outcome determining your future.

Noise is:

The sound of loneliness—of hate

The sound of despair—of pain

The sound of eyes that see no one who loves them

Echoes from tears never shed

Rumbling from tremors never felt

The haunting voices of loves unwanted

Of shame heard—of wisdom put to an agonizing death

Use your voice to reconstruct what you've heard—
your hands to give to others what you've felt.

Create a new note each second;
it will add up to a new great song—
a song with the loveliest melody ever written—the song of you.
The song of you—one long song with ever-changing lyrics—
heard by many, often.
The song of you—recorded by time—able to be heard forever—
a classic masterpiece or never to make the charts.
The choice is yours—you are the creator.

Failure

It's knowing forgiveness—
yet not forgiving.

It's knowing what you want to do—
but doing something else.

It's where you put yourself sometimes,
sealed in a glass jar, not able to communicate
with what you see on the outside.

It's not using the talents given to you,
because you think they won't be accepted properly.

It's those who have consumed all
that they can get their hands on.

It's those who have tolerated no one
who did not live up to their own best interests.

It's those who have the power to make a difference,
blocking from their minds, any idea or item that is meant
to replace something no longer appropriate.

Each day spent—when during that time period
you have not motivated someone to care for you
or to love you.

Each failure should propel you
toward a greater success.

You have failed if—

You hear a worthwhile challenge in your mind
and just continue to sit

The love you feel finds no home

Tolerance and understanding have become
complacency without compassion

There is no room in your heart for a smile

Speaking what you feel
is not important to you

The weight of your life makes you
too heavy to ride the wind

Damn

Damn believing in that
which could never be.

Damn the existence of hurt.

Damn a voice never heard.

Damn war and hatred cleverly disguised
as proper and holy.

Damn prosperity in a basket—
arranged for a picnic—celebrated on a blanket of greed.

Damn all witnesses to the slander of compassion.

Damn darkness, for light is in your eyes.

Damn the wine, for it was not taken.

Damn the stairways that lead to sunsets,
empty because they are not escalators.

Damn the smiles of each existence,
for they show themselves not enough.

Damn creation—leaving much to chance
it will end in exhaustion.

Damn the looseness of a fiber—
not able to hold itself together.

Damn the speech that speaks in circles.
Worse are the hands that applaud it.

Damn each second without forgiveness.

Damn a desire not realized—a dream never seen.

Damn the rapid travelers who never see the sights.

Damn the voices who speak only one rhythm.

Damn a circular sidewalk buried in footprints.

Damn the untruth—worshiped.

Damn all those who are considered
proper for not knowing what really is.

Damn all desires not used
and all wishes not fulfilled.

Damn the tears shed in vain.

Damn the alarm never set
when the time had come to stop.

Damn the stone bridge to freedom that was never built.

Damn the shadows of time that failed to exist.

Damn the existence that failed to leave a mark.

Believe

You were created so that others can put their faith in you.
You exist on the faith you have in others.
You're rewarded by gifts from special carriers dressed
in garments you're not able to wear.

Believe in **quiet mornings**—
birds delivering messages of friendship.

Believe in the mist-laden cloud cover—
wrapping you in a blanket of **love.**

Believe in **a child**—wisdom possessed—
needing only love to smile.

Believe in your life—a breath taken—a thought given.

Believe in **companionship**—
together moment by moment—sharing.

Believe in **strength**—tomorrow stronger than today—
this very moment teeming with opportunity.

Believe in **judgment**—decisions because you have examined
yourself—support yourself with fulfillment.

Believe in **love**—wish for it always—be patient.

Believe in **your fantasies**—for realities are their offspring. Look into all fantasies you believe in; caution is a fantasy.

Believe in **each of your nights**— find bright images in each sound you hear.

Believe in **quality of time**—no one life has enough time for quantity measurements—no one the wisdom to sort and analyze all the pages.

Believe in faith in yourself— in your children—in tomorrow.

Believe in **hope**—fill each second of time and space with hope, patience, and love.

*Believe in **looking up into the sky**—up into time— into the lives that surround you. Believe in **the truth.** Lies are not made from lasting ingredients—the truth is made from pieces of the future.*

*Believe in the **best in all people**—their eyes—their touch. Your inner feelings will tell you who's real for you— who belongs with you—who must not stay.*

Believe in **times to come.** Know where you're going—give yourself time to get there.

Believe in **what's real**—don't expect rivers to run backward.

Believe in the **faith you have in trust**—trust the faith you have.

Ability

Everything within you
has the ability
to move—to solidify—to condense—
to terminate—
to create—
and to fragment.

A spinning world, a moving universe
Plants and more seeds from one simple seed
Children and more children from one simple child
Thoughts and memories from one simple mind
Desires and emotions from one simple being

It all comes together for you every second—
and at that second another you is in its very earliest form.

Ability—Security—Vulnerable

Ability—Energy—Withdrawn

Ability—Trust—Wisdom

Ability—Love—Caring

Ability—Listen—Understanding

Ability—Forgiveness—Compassion

Ability—Challenge—Dream

Ability—Cry—Laugh

Ability—Create—Nurture

Ability—Teach—Learn

Ability—Listen—Understand

Ability—Destroy—Build

Ability—Touch—Ignore

Ability—Follow—Lead

Ability—Change—Accept

Ability—Everything—Nothing

You have the ability to affect it all.
Search for the truth; never again be satisfied to be
a representative of anything less than the truth.
You have the ability to constantly build
the best person you can be.

Think

Breathe deeply—

Breathe deeply—

Breathe deeply—

Relax and think—

Of a casual walk on a sunny day

Of being a kid again

Of having a conversation with your very best friend

Of rain gently dripping from leaves

Of your favorite foods

Think of all things being connected.

Relax and think—

Of covering yourself with a blanket of blue heaven

Of soaring like a bird

Of sandy beaches below your feet

Of mist that falls from ocean waves

Relax and think—

Of being inspired

Of going to the next level

Of eagles perched on mountain peaks

Of creating the perfect day for you

Of music that fills your soul

Of soft hands and a gentle touch

Wake up everyday to the best day of your life.

Think of life as a deep breath in the cold winter air.

Think of time as something that travels with you, not something you're racing against.

Think

Think of "inside you" as a sacred space and all things there in perfect balance.

Think of all things being connected.

?Smile

Smile at conflict and stress

Smile at yourself.

Smile with yourself

Smile at every kind face you see

Smile at the sunrise and sunset

Smile at that which is ridiculous

When you least feel like it—

smile!

Smile at your memories

Smile at every passing glance

Smile at your reflections—they'll return the smile

Smile at your dreams

Greet every challenge
with a smile.

Smile at fear
Smile at your mistakes
Smile at your patience
Smile about your understanding

Don't forget to smile at everything
that makes you smile.

Smile with friendship
Smile with forgiveness
Smile with hope
Smile with love
Smile with gratitude
Smile with grace.

Smile at the sight of boundaries you must cross.

Make sure the paths you follow
are filled with smiles

Smile Right Now!

?Dream

Dream that you have
one—maybe two—come true.

A dream is a lasting, realistic, and often energetic
plan that consists only of thought.

It's a fog-covered book with
missing chapters.

A dream is the mind, free to think and relate thoughts
back to itself in a mystical world
of almost fact.

It's something to do while sleeping—
only to awake and find your
entire life is living this word.

A dream is a shadow as it is
cast forth from and follows you.

A dream is a tender touch by a hand with no face.

A dream is a symbolic gathering
of persons, places, and things in
an uncertain manner.

A dream is what you live in and for—
it grows as you grow.

A dream is reality with a silk veil.
It's you, your surroundings,
the environment that your surroundings exist in.
It's the world that environment has become.

You dream in mostly irregular patterns,
shifting back and forth to find some sort of comfort zone,
some common ground where
you're able to come to terms with reality.
Never have you found it.
Continue to dream and you shall.

Dream of wine and roses

Dream of hills covered with flowers

Dream of a distant shore

Dream of something that almost
happened to you—or did it

Look to the sky to dream, but remember,
dreams are also found on the earth.

?Rainbows

Allow yourself to **walk on rainbows,**
frequently pausing to look at what's beyond.

Your eyes—ever-changing expressions
that often run together—
you're something never seen before.

Climbing midway up the **arch of life** should
seem as flat ground to you—no trees, no rocks—
no mountains—no insurmountable obstacles—
nothing in your way that
can't be overcome.

It's your **walk through life—**
conquering darkness—
painting rainbows.
At times you will be surrounded
by a dense fog of colors
with their magic ability to touch deep inside of you,
creating three dimensional visions.
Let your imagination unfold
before your eyes.
Let you unfold before your eyes.

As you reach the top of your rainbow
continue to walk, not run.
The way down will be a difficult one, but you will prevail.
There is a halfway point of your downward trip.
There colors and images of gold will flash,
occasionally splitting all other colors and piercing your eyes.
Continue to move forward—**your reward is not far now.**

The reward is closer now and your pace quickens.
All the colors go by faster—images from your imagination
now fading into nonsense.
Move faster; let your steps match the beat of your heart.
Distractions will be everywhere, but you must walk on by.

Toward the downside of your rainbow
the mist of color seems to subside—
as if you've come out of a fog.
Everything in front of you seems to be clearing up.
Reality lies ahead.

Reaching the end of your rainbow may prove to be your starting line;
the road leading under the rainbow
provides you with more
than traveling the rainbow itself.

Rainbows show you the way to that
which is precious: to memories—to second chances—
to **the pot of gold known as you.**
Rainbows give you a chance to walk down
a path of sunlight leading to yourself,
passing under the spectrum of
color and into **infinity.**

Return

Returns are joyous;
they are sad.
They can be fantasy.
They can be frequent;
they can be rare.

Come back from a distant place—
ride waves of magic turquoise water to a familiar shore.
Songs from the heavens guide you to your destination.
Returning from a brief memory, guided back by gulls
stretching their wings to produce the wind currents you ride.

Return from the past eager for the future—
caring in your heart—fire in your words—
life in your spirit—spirit in your life.

Return from glory with love inside—
your light will be visible throughout
the cosmos.

If you return a smile,
the image will be with you forever.

If you return a touch,
you will feel it forever.

If you return a look,
you will be seen forever.

If you taste sweetness,
you will cease to be bitter.

If you love each moment,
there will be no sorrow.

Return

Stand on the ground
where you first started—
it's the best place to see
the future clearly

Observe

Find your ladder of life.
Climb to the very top
and gaze out at what is yours—
the valleys you've visited—the high places—
the faces you've known—the loves you've felt.
A lifetime of precious memories known only to you.
The feelings—your experiences—
your happiness—shame—
there has never been and
never will be another you.

While you are you, **let yourself enjoy.**

See yourself as you.
Shed all ornaments, all decorations
given to you by those wishing to make you
into their dream person.

Observe your thoughts.

They shall teach you truth, fairness, and understanding.
Follow the images in your mind.
Focus forever on the destination.
Teach as you learn.
The last look you get of yourself will last forever.
For that reason, keep yourself photogenic.

Imagine that snuggled next to you is a
mirrored image of yourself—living the exact life you desire.
Study it closely. Soon it will begin to fade from sight
and you'll need to carry on the journey alone.

Open your eyes and **see total fulfillment.**
See yourself as part all things—
as total master of your thinking.

That which you conquer today
will help you find new discoveries tomorrow.

Observe nature closely;
protect it, for without it you will become
old and feeble and die before your death.

From a convienent launching pad,
send your mind into orbit around the planet.
Observe—learn from what you see—
adapt to the future you envision.

Guard

Guard yourself against—
Overconfidence
Overindulgence
Overexposure to anything

Guard yourself against—
Running through stop signals
Chasing parked cars
Speeding in the fast lane
Being too cautious

Guard yourself against—
Complacency
Depression
Too many painful situations

Guard yourself against—
Waiting too long for the unresponsive
Total incompetence
Cheaters, liars, thieves
Players who don't play fair
Takers who never plan to give back
Users who throw you away when they're done

Guard yourself against—
Being overstressed
Disease
Gray days
Evil
Hate

Guard yourself against—
Misguided messengers
Inappropriate advances
Birds who fake broken wings

Guard yourself against—
Losing your life balance
Always settling for second best
Approaching *storms, inflexibility*
and *lack of focus*

Guard yourself against—
Overreaction
Twisted memories
Caring about things you really
don't care about

Guard yourself against—
Not being restless
Sleeping too long
Not thinking that life
is too short.

Guard yourself against these things, but—
Protect others when you're able

Kingdom?

Everything—*Everywhere*—has become for you—
your Kingdom.

Laugh lines in a face that cries too often.
Deadlines in a world that moves too fast.
Headlines from a newspaper of only thought.
Communication lines connecting everywhere to you.

Airlines of your mind—
allowing you the freedom to seek understanding.
Pipelines carrying information in both directions.

A place where serenity is you.

Be sweet—be kind.

Be a person of total emptiness
from giving so much.
Rejuvenate from a place
deep within—then give again.

Offer yourself cups of gold

filled with the ***purity*** of the day—

Drink the potion—**Ready yourself**

to enter other kingdoms filled with impurities.

Be strong—make yourself known by your values—

live fast and well.

Labor until you can no more.

Timberlines of life limit your potential—

move past them.

Acquire and **consume great amounts of knowledge—**

to be used later when at last you're able

to ponder and rest amid shining spheres

of white light.

At that moment you'll open your eyes

and know you have obtained forever

the power and glory

needed to carry you forever into a special place

you've created ***inside yourself.***

Your Kingdom

Key

You have the key to doors never opened.

You are the only lock on others.

Doors unopened are worlds never seen—

wisdom never gained—memories vanished.

Open doors wide
that have desires and dreams inside.

Open doors wide that guard the truth.

Open doors wide
that provide you with harmony.

Open doors wide that help you to listen.

Open doors wide that honor your respect.

Open doors wide that comfort you with love.

There are no limits on the number of keys available to you.
Each one opening a new lock.
Work harder to open locks that have rusted due to neglect.
Have patience; pause with each victory, with each new door opened.

Carefully select doors that are meant for you to open.
If your key does not fit, do not force the lock—**move on.**

If victories are open doors that you enter, **stand on firm ground** without movement for a moment before taking a step forward.

Keys to life open doors to freedom and
answer "why," "what will be," and "what has been."
Keys of life open doors to memories and change—
to happiness, to health, to heaven and beyond.
Keys of life open doors to tolerance and understanding—
and to the understanding of who you are.

Search and you'll find keys to doors you never knew existed.

Search and you'll find keys to sunshine felt—to rain heard—to words spoken—to the **universe and beyond.**

The shape of all keys is formed in your heart—by your thoughts.
Each key exists but once. Never are there two exactly the same.
No doors open with the same key twice.
Treat every key as gold. Protect it until you can use it.

Preserve?

Live and preserve life—
the night—your eyes—your soul.
Be all you are to everything.
Be forever free to strengthen
and keep greatness alive—**forever.**

The rights of a world all locked together
and sealed in a glass jar,
with a wax coating and airtight lid
to keep out all that would spoil the contents.

The exactness and beauty of something that is of today—
and how you will do almost anything
to make it last until tomorrow.

When beauty becomes a spectacle
and exactness becomes commonplace.
Save the moment.

Kindness—
dedication—love—
tenderness—caring—
feelings you must preserve.

PRESERVE

The memories of happy times—
of faces with stories—of people who speak
of what really is—of those who dared to be different
when sameness was encouraged.

The memories of quiet back roads and fishing holes—
thoughts of those gone.
Times retrieved by memories—
moments preserved in the mind—
events that have taken place so you might arrive
at the destination that was destiny.

You may always see right
for you remember seeing wrong.

Walk in fields of lazy memories.
During the worst of times think of the finest of events.

Don't let the nature you see decay and die
like the monuments you've constructed.

Kneel down in the tall grasses—
conceal yourself from the winds—
look up to great billowing clouds—
propel your love to somewhere that will be forever.
Be an ally with joy—
and make sure truth surrounds you all the time.

Eat?

Gluttons.

Diets and vegetarians.

Farmers.

Butchers and diabetics.

Peaches and ice cream.

Just plain grub.

Organic.

Ranchers.

Food stuffed, canned, pickled, preserved,

marinated, sautéed,

and garnished.

It's the devouring—the sipping—

the sustenance allowing you

to live another

experience.

It's a Day Stew.

1 cup health
1 cup sickness
1000 slices of happiness
3 ounces of peace of mind
2 stalks of frustration
5 wedges of ambition
1 head of understanding
1 tablespoon of fear
A pinch of hatred
A sliver of jealousy
1/2 cup compassion
1 5-pound package of love
1 large package of faith
1 medium-size can of rejection
Dash of real acceptance
1 cold cup of sorrow
6 to 8 teaspoons of truth
3/4 cup of tears
1 3-ounce can uncut forgiveness
3 cups hope
1/2 cup grated tolerance
2 dashes astonishment
3/4 cup honor
Pinch of shame
4 1/2 cups pride
1/2 cup self conceit
1 clove privacy—minced
Dash of courtesy
1 tablespoon generosity
Pinch of gratitude
1/3 cup finely chopped patience

Fill your mixing bowl one half full with average persons. Sir together slowly until they separate into distinct groups. Using caution, place a best friend type into each group. Add all other ingredients as quickly as possible showing no favoritism for any group. Cover and simmer (don't boil) for five minutes. Remove from heat. Let set for fifteen minutes.

Serves one person for one day.

Note: After twenty-four hours, original ingredients spoil and must be replenished.

?Shell

The sounds of life—of death—
of everything happening throughout history
located within a shell.
Pick it up, put it to your ear, and listen.
You can hear the movement of time.

Your world—freedoms you have and those you don't—
all wrapped into your shell—
the shell that **protects** you from that
which is undesirable.
Watch that your shell doesn't keep out people
and events that you should really **experience.**

It's your weapon—your ***defense.***
The world goes on around you.
Does the opening in your shell face
only that which is desirable to you?

Step outside your shell and—

Scale white mountains
Climb green trees
Speak to unknown faces
Love the display of your feelings
Pray without a prepared text
Cry from within
Touch those who reach for you
Listen to words with meaning
Create new smiles for you to see
Deliver the positive to those who are negative
Break from dormancy, shame, and fear.
Maintain a clear path throughout time.

Stand tall in the dry mild breezes of your life—***feel the future.***
Proceed as you are, your vulnerability guarded—
your abilities non-offensive.
Sleep well in thoughts of security.
Awake into a world you have helped to create.
Live and love inside and out.

The bravery of each of your positive actions
will be **rewarded by medals**
from the greatest of all armies.

He

He **made the world**—created his universe.
Now he rests in a special place
with a spectacular view of everything.

He makes jokes, laughs.
He cries.
He moves with awesome speed and power.
He protects love and touches loneliness.

He *embarks on fantastic journeys into places*
known only to him—some places not yet created,
a future that has not yet happened.

He holds up an hourglass.
Only he is able to view the remaining sand.

He works until exhausted—
carving, shaping thoughts and desires.

He delivers messages through voices we've all heard;
he lives in the eyes of those you have seen.

He knows of rain, wind,
and emptiness not yet imagined.

He knows of commands and
the punishments for not following them.

He knows of terror and fear—by nations and descendants
who build stone pillars for protection.

He has married all who have seen him
and has **helped to carry their burdens.**

He knows of lives saved.
He knows of angels who keep you from harm.

He knows of seven days and of
the celebration of festivals.

He knows of fathers and mothers and of flesh and blood—
of broken chains and walking with dignity.

He knows of the census and of laws.
He hears all that is said, sees what has been done.

He knows of decisions without appeal,
of sentences fully executed—
of false prophets and of your boundaries.
He knows of dust and ashes and seats of honor.
He protects his own and silences the wicked in darkness.

He

He knows of miracles and of justice, of magnificent
chariot races and he's watched the things he loves be destroyed.

He knows what it is to have you hide in him
and use his name without permission—
and to have waves of death surround him.
He knows of hell and distress—of smoke and fire in the jaws
of the heavens.

He knows of dark clouds and the songs of the wind—
of being surrounded by darkness and of an earth
radiant with his own brightness.

He knows of those in trouble and of the perfect way—
of guidance in order to reach the correct path.
He shields all behind him and
shows mercy to anyone truly searching for it.

He knows of the time to celebrate with
a hearty meal and when to send presents to those in need.

He gives wisdom and instruction
and knows you have found substitutes.

He gently paws the earth and the universe
and ***rejoices in his own strength.***

He leads you safely along the top of the cliffs and ridges of life
and holds you safely out of reach of your enemies.
He loves those who hate evil and knows that fairness
is the touchstone of everything.

He knows that an angry man is silenced by
a gift given and a wise man learns by listening—
He knows that kindness makes a man attractive and that a
youngster's heart is filled with rebellion.

He knows of a serene, pleasant summer day
and of lovely autumn mornings during harvest time.

He knows that children suffer from
their father's lack of wisdom.

He knows his own anger rages like a mighty wind
and shall occasionally sweep away shame and false idols.
He feels the land not producing for it is filled with sadness
while living things grow sick and wither away.

He knows some *love melts away* like morning clouds,
then disappears like dew.

He knows You.

He is You.

She

She cradles a nest of new arrivals into all existence.

She **protects and nurtures the new,**
each uniquely separate from the rest.

She prepares a side for you to face
when a ***softer voice*** needs to be heard.

She shapes his lips into her own—
and molds a cheekbone for her comfort.

She sees things she chooses to view—
and speaks on specific topics with insight only known to her.

She moves through time as a rolling mist—changing shape
to match the events around her space.

She charts a course never taking her away from where
she will be needed and blesses those who labor to
smooth out the roads she must travel.

She knows when she alone has the power
and the obligation to speak clearly and with finality.

She knows that she will appear strange to some
who expect to see her other side.

She is durable—and has taught the deaf to hear words never spoken.

She has made a better world, using hands too soft to touch.
She displays time on a dial only she has seen, that only she can read.
She labors with patience to create a tomorrow and enable "now" to be more

She lives infinitely and
speaks with a voice of unmatched quality, clarity, and power.

She knows the names of all sons and daughters,
for she has named them.

She abounds in light and, with the flare she carries, she may warm the sun.

She acts as a midwife between your lives—
and provides each and every provision you'll need during your journey.

She knows of dry ground in the sea and
being sold as a slave in a market now nonexistent.

She knows that golden rings and blue ribbons can skillfully
be clasped together to become a tabernacle.

She has given you tenant lease on today.

She loves both you and your children and
she sees through all the years—
enjoying the celebrations while warning the stubborn and misguided.
She knows of the angry and jealous—
consuming all the earth available to them—
and the valueless compassion offered to their enemies and captives.

She knows of salt seas and coastal plains—
of hordes of families living long and hardy lives together.

?She

She knows that in order for her presence to be felt,
she must embrace all spoken and physical languages.

She knows of a message given to you long ago that has
never been forgotten yet is seldom followed.

She knows of faith.

She knows you must be punished for lying—or be declared innocent.

She knows it's time for great celebrations
because you have both heard and understood her words.

She knows of hidden faults and hearts that know no fear.
She knows of best friends that have turned
against you and of songs that seemed to be written especially for you.

She knows of the earth—melting into submission—feels the pity for the weak and needy and gives them constant care until they have honor.

She knows of a new life—born to replenish all living things—and that her real children will be honored everywhere.

She ***sings lullabies to leaders of men—***
and to poisonous snakes to sooth their violence.

She knows that the wise youth will not
sleep away their hour of opportunity.

She provides you with a deep strength
and your children a refuge and security.

She knows of coin tosses to control decisions and that kind words
are as rewarding and healthful as the most natural of foods.

She knows that *wisdom has more value than foolishness*
and that light is far better than darkness.

She knows of your mistakes and leads you back
to the trail where you made the wrong turn.

She knows that evil will not be tolerated and that the wicked
will be be chased down dark and treacherous tunnels.

She leaves her door open to strangers
but should they abuse her they shall die in shame.

She fills your cup with the sweet gold of life.
You are her visions—her fantasies.

She will gladly unlock the bars of each gate you must pass through.
She will treasure you. She will hope to shine in your darkness.
She will carry you when your legs cannot move.
She will make you comfortable and grateful. She will fulfill her
promises. She will provide a storm too fierce to fight against or
she will allow you to see the beauty and glory
of the moon, stars, and heaven.

She knows You.

She is You.

Love

If you had one —only one—moment,
would you spend most of it on love?

It's a bright sun, warming your body while hurting your eyes—
take the good with the bad.

It's a careful step over a tiny puddle—
a time to be *cautious.*

It's a raging fire giving off rain rather than smoke—
rarely makes any good sense.

It's a piece of wire that you're not able to bend—
makes you less flexible.

It's a piece of ice that is too hot to touch—
something you've not felt before
and might not feel again.

It's a nice day without any people—
a lonesome feeling sometimes.

It's a hand of fingers with too much to touch—
a new world of wonderment and appreciation.

It's a long fuse connected to a short one—
renewed tolerance.

It's a parallel line connected to a circle—
a time to straighten out before entering back into reality.

It's a smile connected to an ear and an eye
reflected by a frown—
a time to be really happy
but *sensitive to what's real and what's not.*

There is a never-ending hunger for love.

Without it—

You have no **breath in your lungs**
You sleep with **no dreams**
You are **empty inside**
You **lack direction and purpose**
You **lose track of your memories**
Your **courage fails**
You **fail to see the beauty in most things**
Your **self-esteem** fades from view
You **become someone you are not**

Happy

On the top of the world,
looking down at creation,
gazing across time and space
to a dawn that
comes to you only once—
the beginning of a **New Day.**

It's where your mind travels to when
it's allowed to be **free.**

A moment—a time—a space filled
by more **good** than you thought possible.

Happiness is an event—
too real to imagine
too emotional to appreciate immediately
never easy to acquire

EVERYTHING CONTAINS
LITTLE VALUE WITHOUT HAPPINESS.

Run and hide from unhappiness.
Play games with your heart and soul—
do not allow unhappiness to enter.
Write words on spaces of visual importance
so as to call attention to your continual search
for **happiness.**

Join together and proclaim unhappiness to be forbidden and nonexistent.

Work every minute at being happy.

Work every minute at making others happy.

Work every minute at changing that which is not projecting happiness into something that provides inspiration for all.

Develop a happy image for yourself—a memory—a person—
a place—a thing—something that every time
you think of it you have a chance to smile.
Then use your happy image every day, as often as possible.

Find enough peace to make your own weather—
sway easy with your moods.

Happiness is giving.

Home

Set up your home to teach these things to all who visit—

Be patient with yourself

Plan to finish before you start

Speak quietly and **balance** all things

Listen to every worthwhile word spoken

Live naturally

Run both with and against the wind

Be strong against wickedness

Never allow wickedness to win over innocence

Stand tall enough to see over the heads of the defeated

Seek out the unfortunate and offer help

Consult others and consume their knowledge

Honor those who have given much so you might be

See the riches in others without envy

Build bridges to essential destinations

Make yourself **accessible** to yourself

You are your home.

Be at home everywhere you are.

Make your home **honest** and **real**—
comfortable and **soothing**—
safe and lasting—

Home is a place to store the memories of a lifetime—to rest—

Home is peace and tranquility—neighbors and friends—family.

Where the sky is seldom gray and your heart is well grounded.

Home is there so you can embark on adventure with security.

Home is memories—wishes and needs—
It's a world of hopes—of fulfillment—of dreams come true.

Home is a foundation—building blocks—plans—
hopes and dreams living together in a space
that provides nourishment to all.

Home is a monument surrounded by love—
shared secrets—plans for the future.

Home is your castle.

Please

Please love yourself.

Please be kind to yourself;
indulge yourself with the sweetness of your best qualities.

Please touch and smooth away
the jaggedness and rough edges within your reach.

Please love your neighbor,
if in your heart he's worthy of such a great honor.

Please take from others only
that which is available without depletion.

Please honor someone and something each day;
the day itself is sufficient.

In your memory, please remember
the good things as bigger than life.
Let the bad rattle around in a capped bottle.

Let please never be an order; rather it is an honor.
Let patience allow you to fulfill the plan of your existence—please.
Please hold your head high whenever possible;
pride is meant to be contagious.

Please allow yourself the opportunity to be who you really are
at least once each day; be conscious of you when you are you.

Please lift your hands to your face.
Gently feel the greatness and grandeur of you.
Smile so your hands fill with every thought that's wonderful.

Please watch for clouds of granite surrounded by blue sky.

Please avoid hills too steep to climb—
but if you must climb one now and then,
be well equipped with reason and understanding.

Please live longer than you know you should.

Please pursue a goal to be the strongest person that you know.

Please deliver only orders for things that
have "available now" listed beneath your name.

Please be everywhere—existing in harmony.
Strike only against those without any firm goodness qualities.
Kiss lips. Hold out a hand soft with tenderness.
Be of one family and protect that family with your existence.

Please be in each part more than
was expected in your total existence.

Light

The sky opens.

For an instant a pyramid of light warms all it touches—and you are transported into a time only dreamed of—into a space hoped to be—into an existence similar to all good experiences ever remembered.

Make sure that you've put yourself in a place where there is nothing to break the path of the light.

The light from your passionate feelings brightens those who choose to be enlightened by it.

You may be separated from hope only when despair has been successful for you. The light of the good that is you will be shared only when it is seen—and only those patient enough to look for it will see the vision.

The light you seek is in the spirit of all things.
It is abundant, but often hard to see.

The light of heaven is seen only by those who look toward it—
never will it be at your feet.

Your light will live tomorrow.
The sea awaits your challenge—
the wind your fragrance—the sky your presence.

Your light will live tomorrow.
The earth will provide for you—
friends will comfort you—
your smile will be their reward.

Prepare yourself for brighter days to come.
All darkness will become light—clouds of light will rumble.
Silent lightning bolts will flash across the sky.

Prepare for the light storm by remembering the darkness—
prepare yourself for love—for humility—for understanding—
for compassion—for pain—for forgiveness—
for faith—for life.

Rain?

Teardrops
and the
Sunshine
that follows.

Fresh air—cleansed and given
a fragrance that is unmatched.

Green grass—muddy roads—growth of life—
growth of
your mind—

Rain is life—
It's a day and it's a night
It's the sunshine of life.

The moods of people—

You and the rain are brothers.
You both shift and sway with the turmoil,
bend in the breeze of life, and become soaked
by the downpour of thoughts and actions.

You are the rain—falling through time
and space—impacting that which you touch.

Rain blows free.
We do not count its drops but we measure its total production—
as with you—measured by your time and space—
your happenings—measured by your encounters—
by each second—by each thought.

Rain is a day with a rainbow.

Rain is a tear on a cheek.

Rain is a steady stream of life.

Rain is a storm of anticipation.

Rain is downpour of wisdom and deep thought.

Rain is the rhythm of your heartbeat

Rain is the sound and feeling of heaven.

**Rain can wash away your fears
and make your worries float away.**

Wind

There's a wind that blows across the land.
It never seems to stop; it just changes direction.

It smoothes out the rocks, sings in the trees,
and makes tall prairie grasses dance.

People who have lived in the wind **become strong** because
they have learned to bend with it.

Others who have never experienced the wind
might think those who thrive in it are weak because
they have learned to protect things inside.
They are misguided for thinking so.

When you live in the wind you must be strong.
Eagle feathers have fallen from the sky to keep you warm,
and stars shine above to show the way to all things below.
Honor and shame are part of each day.
Wisdom is in the earth—everyday is a blessing.

Those who always smile cannot be trusted.
You cannot be hugged by those with knives in their hands.
Walking slowly with purpose is better
than running in several directions.

Eyes can tell you everything you need to *hear.*
The wind teaches you to not use others
to get where you're going
but to help others get
where they need to go.
The wind teaches you that you don't cheat your friends—
you help them win.

Every hill is there for a reason—
to stand on so you can see as far as you can.
When you sit in tall prairie grasses you disappear—you sway
with the wind—you become part of the land.
Listen—you can learn much about yourself
from that sound.

You should not live anywhere that the noise around you
does not allow you to hear the wind.
You should not surround yourself with those
who do not allow you to feel the wind.
You should walk down the path
that is most enjoyable.
You should be who you are without apologizing—
without shame.
You should create the wind
with your motions and emotions.
You should smooth the jagged rocks and
create waves when needed.
You should listen to the wind sing your song—
and *dance with the movement.*

?Time

Time is your ally.

It slowly constructs a life wall for you, every block produced
from knowledge, hope, and understanding,
each placed in its exact proper spot.
As the wall reaches skyward it also increases in thickness.
You are building the wall—constructed by a workman
who acts only on instructions from you—
a workman you'll never know,
constructing a wall of time between you and the end.

Time has given you a reprieve—then another—
and still another.
Time forgives but never lies.
You carry your very own container filled with grains of time; use it well, for it cannot be replenished.

Time may destroy you if you are known to it as a fugitive,
one who abuses the time of others.

Time is the journey of your family line—sisters—parents—
grandparents—brothers—and those not yet born.

Time will obey an evening tear—a silent prayer—
and you will be given an opportunity
to be best man at the marriage
of night and morning.

Time has sparkling eyes, love, and a spirit that never forgets. Time has promised to work for all who wish to be its employer.

Time grumbles when it moves several moments
without you as a mate.

Time casts a continuous shadow on the earth—
an unseen gray tint that is lifted only when
a message of respect and forgiveness
reaches the silver wilderness
that you have occasionally dared to travel through.

Time was meant to be one long glorious day
with mighty conversations about miracles and joy.
Time should not be feared.

Time has given you the wisdom and ability
to reach out and muffle the lies of the past.

Music

There are times when
music is everything,
the only thing that exists in the universe.

The magic of its **complexity—**
the complexity of its simplicity—
the moods of its words ruled by the emotions of its music.

Music has **taught the meek to stand tall—**
given us a bonus just when the basics were not enough.

Music is ***within and around us all***—stimulating the heart—
sharpening our sight—clutching at our emotions.

There is **music in everyone**—
placed inside in the beginning and replenished daily.

Your music may not be heard by others,
nor is it always consciously heard by you.
But it's there, rambling and ringing through your body
lifting you up—bringing you down—keeping you even.

You were provided with the words to each and every song
long before they were written.
You are provided with notes and melodies at birth—
and **the music flows** through your body like a fast train.

Music is an **event of the mind**—love—children and cheaters—
desire and flowers.

Music is a heart filled with forgiveness—of fear—of sacrifice.

Music is filled with blue skies and honey—of honor.
Music is a **celebration.** It is obedience—
a place to find sanctuary and security.

Music is courage and guilt. **It is the wine of angels.**

Music is **understanding.** It is yesterday and plans for tomorrow.

Music is **lifetimes**—punishment and blame—of giving up and of survival.

Music is about asking and crying—about the sun, moon, and beyond.

Music is clay that builds statues. It is a moment of happiness.
It is a sense of being triumphant.

Music brings **kindness.** It tells us about the faithful and the naughty.

Music shows us an ocean of colors—and tells us of generations with humility.

Music projects contempt and anguish—conquest and fury.

Music is **tenderness**—caring. It is glory—sorrow—the innocent.

Music is of smoke—of wind and measurements—
of demons, darkness, and illusions.

You hear in your music yourself—wishing—
hoping that the same music is heard by others.
Your spirit dashes about the village of time, constantly seeking an audience for the most unique concert ever held—**the Music of You.**

Music can alter the mood of the world.

?Catch

Catch a glimpse of yourself—
smiling—laughing—admiring yourself as never before.
Catch yourself falling in love with life.

Catch yourself holding out your hand
to reach another who desires your touch.

Catch yourself being proud of who you are,
pleased with the wisdom you've gained and used.

Others will strain to feel the vibrations you give off.
Everyone who sees you will catch a vision of you—
proud, flexible, daring, honorable, humble, swift, complete.

Accept silver spoons used to eat from the ground,
sometimes passing by what's easy
to reach the truth.

Catch today. Propel yourself past destiny into reality.

Catch up with yourself by traveling straight lines;
change directions by traveling in half circles and on crooked lines.

Catch a peek at each moment of time—at people.
Learn to think of good; store bad in iron caskets.
Plant memories with tomorrow's flowers.

Catch a glimpse—at a considerable distance—
of the vindictive.

Look into eyes without depth—eyes that are mirrors.
See the sadness consumed by self destruction.
Then catch the next express that leads you
far away from that place.

Catch a hand full of free air.
Hold it in your mouth—breathe deep.

Catch all good within reach;
station yourself always in position to receive the most.
Give back all possible. Catch freedom and reward
the world with your smile, your patience,
your understanding,
your wisdom,
goodness, forgiveness, pride,
and honor.

Catch life as it passes. Hold on.
Cling to streams of light.
Receive all things as a precious part of you.
Gather in all—be ever alert—catch your future now.

?Universe

Someplace for your mind to leave
every once in awhile

A place for almost everything to happen

Something that is mine, yours, and theirs

A place

for suns to shine
for thoughts to be **thought**
for facts to be **proven**
for lives to be **lived**
for nature to **produce**
for love to be ***loved***
for energy to shine in **darkness**
for eyes to be **winked**
for hands to be **creative**
for us to be **kind**
for us to be **honest**
for us to share in all that has been **created**

One long song, but who are its writer and producer?

A place where **nothing is too great** for the young to conquer—
and the old hope they are not too late to see it conquered.

Everything lies **within something**—infinite and together.
Each and every day we help to make it all work out
for someone else tomorrow—or even the next day.

The Universe

It spills out. It's full to overflowing with magic—with laughter—
with feelings of being lost and alone.

As you share the minutes of your existence,
as you breathe in and out, as you live in the universe
surrounding you, speak in terms of forever.

Optimism. All things are connected to a purpose.
All understanding is linked to a reason. All people are part of all living.
All everywhere is part of your universe.

The Universe

It's **part of everything** that has ever been or will ever be—
your tiny existence wedged into a fine line.
You've become part of the light and shadows existing between
beginning and end. Yours is a curious, precious time—an existence
hardly visible when viewing the entire scope of all existence.

Do not speak in regular patterns. Softly will command
attention—loudly will not be heard at all.

Birth

You are born with **wide eyes—**
a longing—an urge for **greatness.**

You are born ***squirming***—anxious to achieve—
ready to establish yourself
as part of all things that happen.

You are born crying—gasping for air—alive at last.
You, **determined to contribute, determined to succeed—**
hoping and praying each minute for mental tranquility—
hoping for hope—for **wisdom.**

Determined by your creation—the sun, moon, and stars.
You are born into a place in time—
You are born into the waters of the universe—
emerging instantly into the sea of light—
surviving in a warm clear pool of life.
Your visions are placed within yourself,
then cast out in thought and allowed to be revealed
as you prove worthy.

You are born into a garden—with knowledge of evil—
with thoughts of grandeur—encircled by the fruits of your labor—
fed by your own hand.

You are born into a multiplication table with no infinity

You are born into an identity
with no altering or replacement of you possible
utilizing what you are to become who you must be.

You are a life—a story born—
nurtured by time and controlled by destiny.
Your existence was to be—**for what you touch must be done.**

You are the birth of a universal servant—allowed to partake—
be yourself in a celebration of life.

You are born into a face—a complete existence—
able to distinguish itself—allowed to separate itself from all else.

You are born into predetermined memories of someone not yet existing.
The meaning of your life, your worth is of the highest value
to all who follow.

Each day of your life affects all;
your beginning was celebrated in places never to be known to you.

You are born as an **equal,** for the scene of creation
is fixed in place. You are a part of a census, a registration
of all things everywhere, all with caution movement,
all balanced perfectly.
The measurements are always exact;
the weights, measures, and balances for each moment of
your life.

?Young

You are young when—

Clouds fit inside boxes
and smiles mean love

Laughter displays itself
without need for a veil

Restless nights have bright mornings

You are young when—

Fear comes apart and
can be reassembled
into understanding

For achievement
you receive a reward

You are young when—

A strong helping hand guides you over rough spots

Some of your realities are truly fantasies

You learn to share yourself with others

You feel words create more pain than the needle

You are young when—

Tears display the slightest hurt you've suffered

You sing your favorite songs loud and strong

You understand that being young
has nothing to do with age.

Inability means challenge

The purpose in your eyes is clear

You are young when within yourself
your purpose lies resting comfortably.

School

School is in session—
now and always.

Chapter One: You.

Page One: Yesterday.
On that page is the
word **"Memories."**

Page Two: Tomorrow.
On that page is the word **"Hope."**

Page Three: Today.
On that page is written,
"Today springs forth with
special colors never before seen by you.
Today is something to touch, to love.
Today is in your care; you are responsible for the well being of today.
Your repayment will be a better tomorrow."
The teachings of "today" will bring you closer to
graduation.

Some in your class will excel, and others will lag behind.
Some will simply drop out.
Today your class will learn enough
that others will be compelled to join.
Tomorrow's class will be doubled in size, even though
some now present will be expelled.

The liquor of life tempts drinkers and non-drinkers alike.
Some in your class will learn to ignore certain pleasures
so that tomorrow might offer something even greater.

Today you will fear some
for they are radical about their teachings.
Today you must learn to yell more softly
and say the things that must be said.

Seek the truth. Listen to lectures. Contribute when you can.
Answer each question on every exam you take.
If from your assigned seat, you are unable to hear, understand,
or see, move to a better vantage point.
Choose all electives for yourself only.
When you're called on to instruct,
do so to teach others to think for themselves.

School is in session.
No one will tell you that you cannot attend.
In fact, you must attend if you are to graduate from today
with any degree of understanding that
can be applied to tomorrow.

Listen, read, and learn.

Daydream during low points.

?Class

*Sit—stare—open up from daydreams to see and hear the class now in session.
Choose a front seat for all that is shown is not easily visible—
and not all needed to be heard will ever be said.*

*Your lessons will require no homework. There will be no cheating.
No past achievements will exempt you from any part of the class. Smooth talking
will get you no further than those who find it hard to express themselves.
Money and power will buy you no answers.*

*Your facial expressions will not hide your real thoughts.
There will be no supervision—no managers—no presidents—
no captains; all will be equal.*

*This session will seem brief, but it will be total. It's your chance to excel—
your chance to pass the test.*

*During this session you'll listen to the text as it is read—
and when your chapter arrives you'll hear—you'll see—you—
your life—you—graded on your life. Grades for you will be determined by your
life—the present—and your every past moment. Your every future moment
will be determined by your score in this session.*

*Some who are sure that they'll be at the head of the class
shall find only everlasting gloom and the darkness
that they gave to others during their lifetimes.*

*Others shall graduate with honors, move forward with lifetime achievement
awards and move forward as instructors.*

*Work hard to make sure your grades are sufficient to move on—
you don't want to have to repeat the class.*

Your grading system will consist of:

Your wise use of understanding and compassion

Your love of life

Your kindness

Your faith in yourself

Your respect for the feelings of others

Your forgiveness in your heart

Your respect for life—for all things

Your gentle hand when dealing with poverty and pain

Your total hours with a joyful heart

Your care of the helpless, the weak, and the needy

Your heart—its purity

Your pride—not your arrogance

Your daily desire to feel good about yourself

Your patience with those who love you—including yourself

Your faithfulness to those who truly need it

Your treatment of the earth

Your words—how firm they are—how much can they be relied on

Your house—its character—its foundation—its resiliency

You are graded by your life

Acquaintance?

Avoid the dark hallways of loneliness.

Form a friendship with
that which is surrounding you—
allow that friendship to develop
into a love affair.

It's all those shells you've met in your lifetime—
all those people with faces that run together—
for they never allow themselves to be distinguishable—
never apart from the ordinary and never expressing
more than is necessary to achieve something for themselves.
Shells—one over there—one over here—
and still another right next to you.
There they are—people with a protective coating—
who out of necessity have
developed into emotionless, insensitive machines.

It is important to think for a moment of all those
with whom you're merely acquainted.
Is one of those yourself?

Think of everything you'd like to know more about— including yourself.

Become acquainted with:

Every minute of every day

Your favorite color

Something you must achieve

Something outrageous

Become acquainted with:

Risk

Love

Sensitivity

Memories

Dreams

Become acquainted with:

Humility

Acceptance

Compassion

Patience

Tolerance

Giving

Acquaintances

Become acquainted with yourself

Sincere

A slide-rule giving answers

to any and all of your questions

Those hard-to-find individuals
who must watch what they say—
for what they say is actually what they mean

It's what means the most—
what drives you to open up your innermost feelings.
It's finding out more about someone
you thought you already knew.

It's a realistic statement—an unrealistic statement—
a statement of truth—the proclaiming of that which is real—
an announcement of faith and a believing in
something that is good for you and you alone.
Watch who you share it with.

It's the tide that binds—each link of a chain—
a tool used on the mind.
It's a shame to waste it.

Speak with eyes that reflect what they have really seen—
speak thoughts worthy of being listened to.
Never allow yourself to become part
of a space ashamed of sincerity.

It's a thing you guard—
waiting for the right person and moment to share.

It's that thing you're seldom
ready for when confronted.

What was a joke is now very real.

It's a group of words—thoughts—
an important part of who you are exposed to the world.

It's you—vulnerable to the world—
exposed and alone—praying for the right response.

It's a heartfelt expression
of fact looking for a home.

Secret

Everything you've ever said—
all feelings ever known within you—
all thoughts you've had—
all are the secret known as you.
To unravel the secret
is to know everything about you—
everything possible known only to you.

No time remains for those who have told all—
for those who have expended all—
for without hidden treasures you will rust into the future.

No sunlight shall shine through that which is held within too long.

No life grows in the absolute darkness. Only you can create yourself.

Share your secret wisely!

No mist may dampen the very driest places—
especially if they are not known to exist.

Talk to yourself. Paint pictures and reveal
everything you have always wanted to express.

Trust yourself that your innermost secrets will be understood.

By speaking you will listen.

By listening you will speak.

By telling you will be strong.

By trusting you will thrive.

By understanding you will achieve.

By confiding you will learn.

By not participating you will lose.

?Race

Seconds—minutes—hours—

Time

To the moon—**to a personal triumph**—
the freeway—the sidewalks—
don't race to get to a destination
only to arrive without memory of the trip.

Your body pushed to an unbelievable pace—
covering and overcoming a distance
in less time and with more
grace and finesse
than anyone has ever done.

Thousands of cars—all on the same stretch of highway—
all with a single destination—
all ahead, behind, or right on schedule—
all either behind or ahead of you—
all with the exception of you—
traveling either too fast or too slow.

Thousands of tiny bubbles racing downstream
from a magnificent waterfall—
rushing toward deep blue pools dancing in the sunlight—
moving with the sound of each droplet—
alive with a fluid movement—awakened by the wind.

Stand up and smile—***keep smiling***—laugh—be happy—
keep smiling.
Your heart will know when it's time to stop.

The ground does not move beneath the feet of
those who believe that all required laps of life have been completed.

Race—
With time
Without reason
With wisdom
Without logic
With dignity
Without regard
With purpose
Without agendas
With fulfillment
Without motives
With desire
Without necessity
With freedom
Without confinement

Abundance?

There is an abundance of everything,
yet not enough of anything.

What is an adequate amount to some
can be an overwhelming burden to others.

Each person—in his own way—
must obtain the proper measurement
of everything life has to offer,
and at the same time attempt to understand
the needs of others.

Thoughts

Lasting only a moment, a thought streaks through
the mind of that creature known as you.
Memories pulsate a billion beats per minute—streams of thought
from a select few reach into the stationary darkness of time

Thoughts

There they are all caught and stored in a huge glass jar.
Minute by minute more impulses enter the container.
It becomes alive with an abundance of thought and begins to vibrate.
The walls begin to weaken;
slight cracks become visible from the outside.
Still more thoughts enter, though nothing escapes.
The pressure mounts, the cracks widen.

With the rumbling of overload and imminent explosion,
you scurry for far-off shelters and sanctuaries.
The fury inside the walls heightens to such intensity that a shrill
noise is heard by all. Then suddenly, the cataclysmic explosion
of a magnitude previously thought impossible shatters and
disintegrates the protective walls of the container.
Like millions of tiny sand pebbles cast into the bright clear water
of space, the thoughts of all mankind are propelled outward—and
you must start all over again, or you must simply simplify.

Abundance is—

Everything big—*nothing small*

Everything taken in—*nothing given out*
Everything consumed—*nothing returned*
Everything gained—*nothing lost*
Everything lost—*nothing gained*
Everything learned—*nothing remembered*

Life

Live it well!

Contribute all that is necessary to fulfill your dreams.

Live with enthusiasm—with health,
with confidence, with empathy.

Each life is a dream, with a beginning and an end.
A dream with colors and feelings,
with moral fiber, with lessons to be learned,
with dignity, self esteem, humility, and self determination.

Strive to beat all the odds—to become
the person you know you are.

If you were to select a portion of today to add
to your life tomorrow, what would that be?
What is and will be right for your life tomorrow?

**If need be, erase today and start over to
construct your new life tomorrow.**

Life is **born**— you must grow

Life is **air**—you must breathe

Life is a **gift**—you must give

Life is to **ponder**— you must think

Life is **learning**— you must be thoughtful

Life is **growth**— you must achieve

Life is **teaching**—you must contribute

Life is **faith**—you must believe

Life is **challenge**—you must take risks

Life is **pain**—you must retain perspective

Life is **brief**—you must maximize every minute

Life is **joy**—you must share with others
and for others to share with you

Life is you **now,**
using what you've learned
accomplish what you've planned.
Do more for others
and you'll be **giving** more
to the memories of you.

Tomorrow

Tomorrow is a place with
no shape—no sound—no memory.

Tomorrow is a place where past **sadness is not welcome—** where only that which you choose may exist.

Tomorrow is a place where heroes of the past live well.

Tomorrow is time placed beyond an event—
a change and a hope.

Tomorrow arrives—smiling, optimistic, and proud.

Tomorrow is a newborn, not knowing
what is "right" or what is "wrong,"
hungry to learn the wonders of what could be.

Tomorrow seems to linger before its first move.
It should be **cautious.** ***It should hide nothing.***

Tomorrow is a cast of players,
each writing themselves into the day.

Someday, as if by design, a **surprise** to some,
there will be no more tomorrows.
There will be no chance to redeem and no consolation prize
for a poorly played yesterday.
"No Tomorrow" will consist of—no music—
no plans—no fears—no dreams—no memories—
no today—no future—**No You.**

Today should be all you can make it.
The You of Tomorrow will be born
from what already exists Today.

Today's battle scars bring
wisdom to tomorrow.

Today start something new.
Move past any resistance to new ideas.
Set goals in writing.

Tomorrow is conceived, born, and loved by you.
It matures, laughs, cries, feels, touches, learns, dies.

If Tomorrow is to be what you want it to be,
Today should be more.

Why

Why Questions?

Because it all *started as it did*—and has *regressed into what it has become.*

Because we see no mountains with peaks sharp enough to cut the wind.

Because **we're not alive with the enthusiasm** that we had in the past.

Because the cold have become frozen and the hot have expanded.

Because some ***love is given for only selfish reasons.***

Because those who have really seen the light are accused of being blind.

Because we've witnessed miracles with unturned heads.

Because mirrors now reveal only what the viewer would like to see.

Because unreliable sources have pushed themselves
to the front row of respectability.

Because the understanding of true understanding has ceased to exist.

Because **lust and self pity** fly about the air more than the birds.

Because ***disease has become part of our economy.***

Because people unknown by anyone have become everyone's best friend.

Because all good energy has been used twice over.

Because good times are often not much better than the bad.

Because everyone has received a reward—but only a handful realize it.

Because *honesty is seldom the best policy.*

Because hope and fear are too equally balanced in everyone.

Because wickedness and evil are seen through all eyes.

Because the **noise of each second is much too great.**

Because communication between all
has become too difficult for words.

Because in the beginning it was all created.

Because in the beginning the darkness was upon the land.

Because the earth and seas were once looked upon as being good.

Because the sun, stars, and moon were once looked upon as being good.

Because **man was once looked upon as being good.**

**It's a word that when used continually
will connect everything conceivable.**

**It's a word that when used once will connect
everything imaginable.
It's a word that when never used
leaves everything magically believable.**

Published by TSM Publications
P.O. Box 1292
Escondido, California 92033
619.890.4222

Interior and cover design by Charles McStravick, Artichoke Design

ISBN 13: 978-0-615-37330-0

Library of Congress Control Number: 2010928410

Publisher's Cataloging-in-Publication Data
Available upon request

PRINTED IN THE UNITED STATES OF AMERICA

Dedication

To my wife and friend, Vicki,
and to my daughters,
Karen, Christa, Shanda, and Tori.

To all my friends and family—Thanks!

To the memories of those very special people
in my life who are gone.

Acknowledgments

Thanks to Karla Olson of BookStudio.
Her dedication as editor helped *Questions* become a reality.

Thanks to Charles McStravick of Artichoke Design,
for great work on the design of *Questions*.

To order additional copies of
Questions: Directions to Who You Are,
please visit:

www.questionsthebook.com

or

www.amazon.com

Discounts for multiple copies are available.
Please contact the publisher:

TSM Publications
P.O. Box 1292
Escondido, California 92033
619.890.4222

or

tim@questionsthebook.com